HOW DID IT HAF

THE RISE
OF NAZISM

Charles Freeman

W
FRANKLIN WATTS

Sch

D0246014

60 000 052 008

First published in 2005 by Franklin Watts
Reprinted 2007

Copyright © 2005 Arcturus Publishing Limited

Franklin Watts
338 Euston Road, London, NW1 3BH

Franklin Watts Australia
Level 17/207 Kent Street, Sydney, NSW 2000

Produced by Arcturus Publishing Limited
26/27 Bickels Yard, 151–153 Bermondsey Street
London SE1 3HA

Series concept: Alex Woolf
Editor: Rebecca Gerlings
Designer: Stonecastle Graphics
Picture researcher: Thomas Mitchell

Picture credits:
All images copyright of Getty Images

A CIP catalogue record for this book is available
from the British Library

Dewey Decimal Classification Number: 943.085

ISBN: 978-0-7496-7724-4

Printed in China

Franklin Watts is a division of
Hachette Children's Books

Northamptonshire Libraries & Information Service	
60 000 052 008	
Peters	12-May-2010
943.086	£7.99

Contents

1 A Shattered Nation

O n 30 January 1933, Adolf Hitler, leader of the Nazi Party, was made Chancellor of Germany. Central to Nazism was the revival of the power of the German nation. Hitler intended to restore German power by putting into place a political strategy which emphasized to the nation the importance of race, authority and the right of the German people to expand to the east at the expense of the 'inferior' Slav peoples who lived there. Inside the state, political enemies such as the communists and Jews would be eliminated from public life. The full horror of Nazi rule unfolded during the 1930s, until the whole of Europe was at war and the Jewish people were being systematically exterminated.

It had been a weakened Germany that had greeted Armistice Day on 11 November 1918. This ceasefire marked the end of the First World War, one of the most terrible wars in history. For four years the major nations of Europe had poured their men and money into a struggle for supremacy over their continent. The strongest and most efficient of these nations had been Germany – it had fought its huge neighbour Russia to a standstill and throughout the war occupied large parts of northern France. However, despite appalling losses, France, aided by its ally Great Britain, had hung on, holding the Germans to a stand-off in the trenches of the Western Front. With the help of a new ally, the United States, the Allies fought off a final German offensive in the summer of 1918 and the German armies began to retreat. When news came of the collapse of Germany's allies, Bulgaria and Austria-Hungary, morale slumped and the German generals accepted surrender.

It was a terrible shock for the country and humiliation soon followed. The German navy was forced to turn itself over to the Allies, the army was driven back into Germany and a blockade of food supplies kept the population near starvation. The shock was so great that a rumour arose that Germany had not actually been defeated – instead its army had been sabotaged by enemies back home, revolutionaries or Jews. The fact that

In the communist uprisings of 1919, the Royal Palace in the capital, Berlin, was a natural target for looting workers. This is the shattered entrance of the palace. The German middle classes felt so threatened by the uprisings that they were prepared to put their faith in anyone who would restore good order.

VOICES FROM THE PAST
Disillusionment

A soldier returns home to find that traditional German values have been threatened by the defeat:

'Returning home we no longer found an honest German people, but a mob stirred up by its lowest instincts. Whatever virtues were once found among the Germans seemed to have sunk once and for all into the muddy flood ... Promiscuity, shamelessness and corruption ruled supreme...'

Richard Evans, *The Coming of the Third Reich* (Allen Lane, Penguin, 2003)

Germany was never occupied fuelled the belief that defeat had come from the inside. Those who had signed the Armistice became known as 'the November Criminals'. In the chaos the government, which had been under the control of two generals, Paul von Hindenburg and Erich von Ludendorff, disintegrated. Germany's emperor, Kaiser Wilhelm II, fled to Holland.

Restoring Order – the Weimar Constitution

As Germany descended into the chaos of defeat, there were communist uprisings in many major German cities. The workers were inspired by the recent Russian Revolution of 1917 and their temporary success led to panic among the middle classes. Friedrich Ebert,

Friedrich Ebert, the leader of the German Social Democratic Party – a long-established and moderate workers' party – proved to be the saviour of Germany. A firm disciplinarian but also a flexible negotiator, he restored order to the streets and oversaw the drawing up of the Weimar Constitution. Here, he is being sworn in as the party's first president on 11 August 1919.

the leader of the Social Democrats, a moderate workers' party, was able to restore order by 1920 with the help of the army and the *Freikorps*, bands of young men and ex-soldiers formed to help patrol the streets. The Freikorps often lacked discipline, but this was tolerated by the middle classes when communists were the victims of their violence. One result was that street fighting between rival armed bands became a feature of everyday life.

With the return of some stability by 1919, Ebert's government drew up a new constitution. Germany was to be a republic, known as the Weimar Republic after the town where the constitution was drawn up. The Kaiser would not return, and in his place would be a president elected by popular vote every seven years. The centre of power was the parliament, the Reichstag. Elections would be by proportional representation; that is, the electors would vote for their favoured political party, and seats for the deputies, or members of the Reichstag, would be distributed according to the number of votes for each party. If one person in three voted for the Social Democrats, for example, they would receive a third of the seats.

The problem was that there were a large number of political parties. While the Social Democrats, who represented the vast majority of the German workers, wished to work peacefully towards a workers' state, there was also a communist party that still hoped for revolution. The two parties fought with each other over the workers' vote. The Centre Party had close ties with the Catholic Church. Conservatives, especially those in rural areas who yearned for a return to pre-war Germany with its hierarchy of Kaiser and landowners, voted for the National People's Party. These and other smaller parties represented such a range of views that it would be difficult for any party to get a majority. Parties would have to form alliances, or coalitions, with other parties to do so. If the parties of the Reichstag failed to agree, then the president could intervene and rule on his own authority by decree. If order broke down he could bring in the army to restore it. Right from the beginning of the Weimar Republic, it was possible for parliamentary democracy to be bypassed by a strong president.

There was intense anger in Germany when the terms of the Versailles Treaty were made known. Despite every effort to oppose the terms, it soon became clear that Germany would have to sign or risk the renewal of the war. Here are the German delegates gathered at Versailles for the signing.

TURNING POINT

The humiliation of Versailles

On 7 May 1919, the German delegation to Versailles, which had played no part in the negotiations, was given the final text of the treaty to read. Its members were appalled. Back in Germany, many in the army and the government refused to agree to it. 'Germany cannot accept these terms and live with honour as a nation,' said the head of the delegation. But the Allies would not negotiate and threatened to renew the war if Germany did not agree to the treaty. Eventually, the Germans capitulated and on the 28th the delegation signed. 'It was the worst hour of my life,' said one delegate. The German people never forgot the humiliation.

Much of Germany's anger over the Versailles Treaty lay in the loss of so much territory in the east, as shown on this map. East Prussia was, in fact, cut off from the rest of Germany. In the west, Alsace-Lorraine was returned to France and other adjustments were made to the border. The new state of Austria was forbidden to join with Germany.

The Treaty of Versailles

Almost immediately, the republic faced its first test, that of making a peace settlement. Germany's new rulers hoped that since they had established a democracy in place of the military government, the

The First World War was the first war in which air power had been used extensively, largely for reconnaissance. It was clear, however, that planes could also be used for bombing and, as part of the Treaty of Versailles, Germany was forced to disband its airforce. This picture shows the scrapping of those planes which remained.

victorious Allies would not be too harsh towards their defeated nation. However, when the Allies met to draw up a peace treaty at Versailles – the former palace of the kings of France outside Paris – they showed no mercy towards Germany.

The French in particular were hungry for revenge and wanted to punish Germany and cripple its forces. Germany and its allies were declared guilty of causing the war, resulting in Germany having to make a large reparation payment for the damage it had caused. The once proud German army was reduced to 100,000 men and was allowed no aircraft. To make sure France was protected, no German troops at all were to be placed on the Rhineland, the land alongside the French border. The German borders with the new state of Poland, which was carved out of the former Russian empire, were drawn in Poland's favour. All Germany's colonies were to be taken away. Thirteen percent of the country's land and 10 percent of its people were lost. The signing of the Versailles Treaty on 28 June 1919 was a day of humiliation for Germany. Any politician who promised to reverse it would find a ready audience.

HOW DID IT HAPPEN?

The Treaty of Versailles

From the moment it was signed to this day, the debate over whether the treaty was too harsh has continued. The British economist J. M. Keynes argued against the treaty in 1920:

'The policy of reducing Germany to servitude for a generation, of degrading the lives of millions of human beings, and of depriving a whole nation of happiness should be abhorrent and detestable ... Some preach it in the name of justice. In the great events of man's history justice is not so simple.'

A modern view is more supportive of the treaty. 'The Treaty's territorial provisions were mild compared to what Germany would have imposed on the rest of Europe in the event of victory, as the Treaty of Brest-Litovsk, concluded with the Russians in the spring of 1918 had graphically demonstrated ... The reparations bills that Germany actually did have to pay from 1919 onwards were not beyond the country's resources to meet and not unreasonable given the wanton destruction visited upon Belgium and France by the occupying German armies.'

J. M. Keynes, *The Economic Causes of the Peace* (Harcourt, Brace and Howe, 1920); Richard Evans, *The Coming of the Third Reich* (Allen Lane, Penguin, 2003)

This picture, from early June 1919, shows a mass demonstration in Munich against the terms of the Treaty of Versailles. It was in Munich that Hitler founded the Nazi party, which drew very heavily on this discontent.

2 Hitler and the Birth of the Nazi Party

Hitler's *Mein Kampf* was a long, rambling work full of Hitler's obsessions. Within its pages, however, Hitler did set out his plans for European domination. Although few Germans read it, *Mein Kampf* became the bible of the Nazi movement. This finely bound copy, complete with embossed swastika, dates from 1939.

Among the thousands in shock in the defeated Germany of 1918 was a 29-year-old Austrian who had served in the German army. Adolf Hitler was in hospital recovering from the effects of a gas attack. He later described his reaction to the news of Germany's defeat: 'I threw myself on the cot and buried my burning head in the covers ... And so it had all been in vain ... Did all this war happen so that a gang of wretched criminals could lay hands on the fatherland? ... In these nights hatred grew in me, hatred for those responsible for this deed.' Hitler vowed that he would seek out and destroy those who had brought about Germany's defeat.

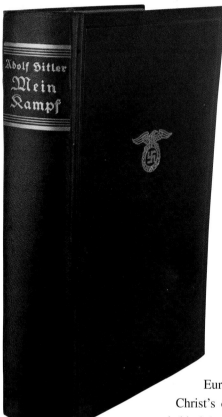

The Young Adolf Hitler

Adolf Hitler had been born in Austria in 1889. His father, Alois, a cold and distant man, was a customs official working on the border between Austria and Germany. Hitler's mother, Klara, was Alois' third wife. She was 23 years younger than he was and dominated by him. Alois died in 1903 and by 1905 Hitler had left home for Vienna, the capital of the Austro-Hungarian empire. He hoped to enter the Academy of Fine Arts to study as an artist, but he was rejected twice and took to a life of drifting in the city. He was deeply affected by the death of his mother from cancer in December 1907.

As he went from one cheap lodging house in Vienna to another, the lonely Hitler brooded on his misfortunes. He described later in his autobiography *Mein Kampf* ('My Struggle') how he gradually came to believe that the Jews were responsible for the evils of the world. Anti-Semitism (deep prejudice against Jews which was based as much on their race as their religion) was common throughout Europe. Many Christians still held the Jews responsible for Christ's death, while others saw Jewish speculators as the power behind the rapid and unsettling industrialization of the age. For Hitler, however, anti-Semitism became an obsession and he stressed the racial inferiority of Jews. He wrote: 'Wherever I went, I now saw Jews, and the more I saw, the more sharply they set themselves apart in my eyes from the rest of humanity … Was there any form of filth or profligacy, particularly in cultural life, without at least one Jew involved in it?'

In 1913, Hitler moved from Austria to Munich, the capital of the southern German state of Bavaria, and it was there that he joined the German army when war was declared in 1914. Although his army

VOICES FROM THE PAST

Hitler's school days

Hitler's teacher Professor Eduard Humer remembers his pupil:

'I can recall the gaunt, pale-faced youth pretty well. He had definite talent, though in a narrow field. But he lacked self-discipline, being notoriously quarrelsome, willful, arrogant and irascible … his enthusiasm for hard work evaporated all too quickly. He reacted with ill-concealed hostility to advice or reproof; at the same time he demanded of his fellow pupils their unqualified subservience, fancying himself in the role of leader.'

Franz Jetzinger, *Hitler's Youth* (Greenwood Press, 1977)

When news of the outbreak of war swept through Europe in August 1914, it was greeted with enthusiasm. Each nation felt that it would have its chance to solve its grievances. Hitler had arrived in Munich from Austria the year before, and this photograph shows him among the crowds in the Odeon Platz in the city.

Although Hitler never rose higher than corporal in the army, his war record was good and he was even awarded an Iron Cross (a medal for distinguished military service) for his bravery. It seems clear that he benefitted socially from the comradeship of army life after his years of loneliness in Vienna. This picture shows him (on the right) together with two fellow soldiers at a military hospital in April 1915.

career was modest – he served as a runner between the trenches – he found some comradeship among his fellow soldiers and was even awarded an Iron Cross.

Hitler Finds a Role

After the war, Hitler, like other Germans, had to adjust to the new Germany. At first he remained a soldier. In Munich the army was being used to check up on the many small revolutionary parties, and in September 1919, Hitler was sent to observe the meeting of a group calling themselves the German Workers' Party. At his first meeting, Hitler intervened so effectively in an argument that he was asked to become a member of the executive committee that ran the party.

After 30 years of obscurity, Hitler suddenly realized he had a gift for public speaking. He sensed the frustrations of the audiences drawn to the German Workers' Party. The Treaty of Versailles had just been signed and the German economy was in chaos. Hitler declared these problems must be the fault of someone, and the German people must be mobilized to fight back, destroy their enemies – among whom

VOICES FROM THE PAST

Exploiting the masses

Hitler tells of his contempt for his audiences. It was the way in which he shamelessly exploited their emotions which made him such a powerful orator:

'The receptivity of the great masses is very limited, their intelligence is small, but their power of forgetting is enormous. In consequence of these facts, all effective propaganda must be limited to a very few points and must harp on these in slogans until the last member of the public understands what you want him to understand by your slogan.'

Adolf Hitler, *Mein Kampf* (Lightning Source UK Ltd., 2004)

Hitler placed Jews and communists – and revive the nation. Over the next few months the numbers drawn by Hitler's oratory grew. People seemed transfixed as they listened to him.

The Nazis Are Formed

In February 1920, the small but growing party was renamed the National Socialist German Workers' Party, a name that its opponents shortened to Nazis. Gradually, the shapeless group of discontented hangers-on became organized. By July 1921, Hitler was clearly leader of the party. He put forward a programme of 25 points, among them the revocation of the Treaty of Versailles, a greater Germany uniting all Germans with enough land to feed all its peoples, and the end of civil rights for Jews. The symbol of the party was the swastika, an ancient sign that was now produced in black, red and white, the colours of the German imperial flag. It was displayed on banners and the armbands of party members.

The SA were typical of many similar armed groups which political parties used to give an image of disciplined good order. In practice, the SA would often behave brutally against rival groups.

The great inflation of 1923 was so serious that the German mark in effect lost its value completely. Prices eventually reached a billion times what they had been in 1914 and, at the height of the inflation, it was impossible to print enough bank notes to keep up with price rises. As this picture shows, piles of notes which had lost their value ended up as toys.

Many of the party's first recruits were drawn from the thousands of disgruntled young men who roamed the streets of Munich. With the Freikorps as the model, the Stormtroopers, or SA, were formed in October 1921 as the shock troops of the Nazis. They wore brown shirts as part of their uniform and were soon used to keep order at meetings. Hitler himself created a team of bodyguards, the SS, or *Schutzstaffel* ('protection squad'). These organizations gave an image of uniformed discipline to the party. At a parade in Munich in January 1923 for instance, 6,000 Stormtroopers attended. As more chaos hit Germany with the great inflation of 1923, this display of order proved attractive, particularly to the middle classes who now formed the majority of the party's members. Nazi membership totalled 55,000 in 1923.

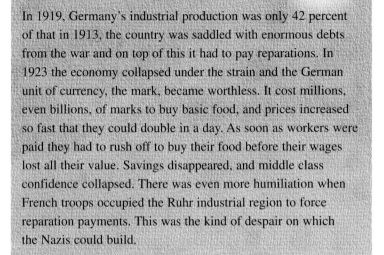

TURNING POINT

The inflation of 1923

In 1919, Germany's industrial production was only 42 percent of that in 1913, the country was saddled with enormous debts from the war and on top of this it had to pay reparations. In 1923 the economy collapsed under the strain and the German unit of currency, the mark, became worthless. It cost millions, even billions, of marks to buy basic food, and prices increased so fast that they could double in a day. As soon as workers were paid they had to rush off to buy their food before their wages lost all their value. Savings disappeared, and middle class confidence collapsed. There was even more humiliation when French troops occupied the Ruhr industrial region to force reparation payments. This was the kind of despair on which the Nazis could build.

Not least of the humiliations following the war was the occupation of the Ruhr – an important industrial region – by French troops, shown here marching into a small German town in January 1923. The sense of humiliation was easy for the Nazis to exploit, and they circulated lurid stories of French brutality.

The Beerhall Putsch

Yet, although the Nazi Party was growing, Hitler had a problem: the Nazis were based in one state, Bavaria, in the south of Germany. This was a long way from the capital, Berlin, where Hitler needed to seize power if he was to achieve control of Germany. There was, however, an example of such an achievement for him to follow. In Italy, the fascist leader Benito Mussolini had built up a movement that was similar to the Nazis. It played on the frustrations left by the First World War and ridiculed the weak Italian government. Its troops were known as the blackshirts and, in October 1922, Mussolini ordered them to march on Rome, Italy's capital, to seize power on behalf of the nation. To everyone's astonishment the Italian government, overcome by political infighting, offered no opposition and Mussolini bullied his way into becoming prime minister.

In November 1923, Hitler planned a similar attack. He would seize the leading members of the Bavarian government (when they were speaking in a Munich beerhall) and force them to march with him on Berlin. He persuaded the First World War general Erich von Ludendorff to join him.

The *Putsch*, or attempt to seize power, was a fiasco. The Bavarian ministers were captured but then escaped. When the

The Beerhall Putsch of November 1923 failed because of poor leadership and planning. Here, holding the flag, Heinrich Himmler – later the head of the SS – and Stormtroopers man a barricade by the Bavarian War Ministry as the coup gets under way. The Stormtroopers were easily dispersed by the police.

HOW DID IT HAPPEN?

The key role of Hitler

Historians disagree as to whether it was Hitler's unique gifts that led to the rise of Nazism or whether it was the failure of the Weimar Republic to establish legitimacy among the German people.

The journalist Konrad Heiden sums up the way Hitler sensed the needs of the masses and how he promised to meet those needs:

'With unerring sureness, Hitler expressed the speechless panic of the masses faced by an invisible enemy and gave the nameless spectre a name … His speeches are the daydreams of the soul of these masses … they always begin with deep pessimism and end in overjoyed redemption, a triumphant, happy ending … This makes him the greatest mass orator of the age.'

Other historians have argued that the failure of the Weimar Republic to put down democratic roots left the way open for the Nazis:

'After the First World War a strong government which had the entire population behind it was absent from German politics. Weimar governments lacked the basis of support and popular legitimacy to push through unpleasant but necessary measures democratically – a failure which led to the hyperinflation of 1922–3 … the painful measures taken to introduce a stable currency rested on emergency measures which bypassed the Reichstag.'

Historian Richard Bessel in Ian Kershaw (ed.), *Why did Weimar Democracy Fail?* (Weidenfeld and Nicolson, 1990)

Hitler's experience in Landsberg prison, where he stayed less than a year in 1924, was not a harsh one. His cell was bright and airy and he was allowed visitors. Some 500 came altogether. During his stay, he completed *Mein Kampf*, his autobiography. Here Hitler is pictured looking out from his cell. The picture was sold to Nazi supporters as a postcard.

Stormtroopers took to the streets of Munich they were fired on by the police. Hitler had to flee.

Despite the defeat, when Hitler was put on trial for treason he realized that the trial would be reported across the nation and could be used as a platform for the Nazi cause. He proclaimed that he had only been fighting for Germany, and aroused such support that the court sentenced him to only five years in prison. He did not serve even that and was released within a year. Yet, in 1924, with the Nazis gaining only 3 percent of the vote in the Reichstag elections, his campaign for power seemed to be stalled.

3 The Years of Frustration: 1924–9

When Hitler was released from prison in December 1924, his party seemed to be in ruins. Without his leadership it had split into quarrelling factions. It was even banned completely in Bavaria. Yet Hitler was not daunted. His time in prison had only strengthened his belief that he would be the saviour of Germany, and he made plans to revive the Nazis. By early 1925 he had had the ban on the party lifted.

The revival of the Nazi Party after 1925 involved extending the party to the young. The Hitler Youth was formed in 1926. There was a strong emphasis on flags and marching as this picture of a Hitler Youth group shows.

VOICES FROM THE PAST

Hitler's change of strategy

In 1925, after the failure of the Beerhall Putsch, Hitler accepted that the only path to power lay in parliamentary elections:

'When I resume work it will be necessary to pursue a new policy. Instead of working to achieve power through an armed coup, we shall have to hold our noses and enter the Reichstag against the Catholic and communist deputies. If out-voting them takes longer than out-shooting them, at least the result will be guaranteed by the Weimar Constitution. Any lawful process is slow … Sooner or later we will have a majority … and after that … Germany.'

K. Luedecke, *I Knew Hitler* (E. Scribner's Sons, 1938)

Imposing Control

Hitler had learned from the failure of the Beerhall Putsch that he would have to work for power through the Reichstag elections. The voting system of the Weimar Constitution made it possible for even small parties to win a few seats but only a well organized nationwide party could hope to achieve national success. There had to be an undisputed leader and a clear programme enforceable throughout Germany. One obstacle was the Strasser brothers, Gregor and Otto, whom Hitler had sent to start up party branches in the northern industrial cities of Germany. There was a risk that the Strassers would build their own power bases free from Hitler's control. Meanwhile, in the Rhineland, another rising Nazi, Joseph Goebbels, was proving to be almost as talented a public speaker as Hitler himself.

In 1926, Hitler finally moved in on his rivals. Goebbels was won over after being harangued by Hitler and soon became one of Hitler's most devoted followers. When placed in charge of the party in Berlin, he developed into the most brilliant and unscrupulous propagandist in the party. He instinctively knew which lies about his opponents were most likely to be believed and how to use his local Stormtroopers to beat up the Nazis' enemies, while saying it was all in the name of keeping good order. Gregor Strasser was also confronted, told directly by Hitler that many of his policies were nonsense, and forced to accept Hitler's leadership.

A National Party

Hitler could now put in place a national organization. To allow Nazis to run in elections, party headquarters were set up in each of the 35 electoral regions into which Germany was divided. These were linked to local branches. There were many opportunities for local leaders to emerge so long as they swore their allegiance to Hitler. Hitler, in fact, liked to see young Nazis fighting to control their local

This picture from 1928 shows Hitler meeting a group of Hitler Youth members and Stormtroopers at the SA headquarters in Munich. The swastika armband was worn as a compulsory part of the Nazi uniform.

TURNING POINT

Hitler enforces his leadership

In 1925 and 1926, the Nazi Party was beginning to expand outside Bavaria. It could easily have split into numerous small parties with local leaders challenging Hitler's control. Already some Nazis were complaining that the Austrian Hitler was not even a proper German. Hitler had to act decisively. He bullied his rivals into submission, offering them good posts if they would accept his leadership completely. Then at a party rally in July 1926, the Stormtroopers were made to swear oaths of loyalty to the leader as they marched past him, with their right hands stretched towards him in what was now a compulsory salute. There were no more threats to Hitler's leadership and some Nazis even began to talk of him as if he were divine.

The German peasant farmers, here a group of women with an asparagus crop in the early 1930s, suffered badly in the Depression. The Nazis played on their insecurities with promises that they would support the ancient relationship of farmers with the German soil. The party was soon winning a high proportion of votes in the rural areas of northern Germany.

parties as it confirmed his ideas that life was a continual struggle in which only the fittest would come to the top. It was certainly true that many able and well-educated young men were drawn into the party. Over 90 percent of the members of the Nazi party were male: for Nazis, a woman's place was in the home.

In order to attract supporters at a young age and to build up future recruits for the Stormtoopers, the Hitler Youth movement was founded in 1926. The Hitler Youth was a logical extension of Hitler's belief that the future of Nazi Germany lay in its children and that the party should be as influential in their education as their schools. There were separate organizations for boys and girls: the boys' section prepared them for military service, the girls' for motherhood.

Hand in hand with the growth of a national expansion of the party came the support of groups it had not reached before. One of these was the small peasant farmers of northern Germany. The inflation of 1923 had been followed by falling prices that had forced many farmers into bankruptcy. The Nazis cunningly told the farmers that their honest toil on the land made them the core of Germany; there was much talk of German 'blood and soil', and promises of help if the Nazis came to power. By 1928, nearly 20 percent of the votes in some rural areas were going to the Nazis at a time when they still almost had no support at all in the big cities.

Stalemate

The Nazi Party thrived when times were hard for the people of Germany. Desperate and unsettled, the Germans were all the more responsive to the Nazis' promise, outlined in 1921 in the programme of 25 points, to destroy the Treaty of Versailles, revive Germany through a policy of expansion to the east and deprive the Jews of civil rights.

Hitler was adept at reaching out to other movements which might support the Nazi programme. Here he is shown meeting in August 1927 with leaders of the National People's Party, who were in sympathy with many of his aims.

Yet the attractions of these policies eventually faded. After 1924, the German economy stabilized and actually began to grow. Investment began to pour in, especially from the United States, and an energetic foreign minister, Gustav Stresemann, worked hard to improve Germany's relations with its old enemies. An ardent nationalist, he realized that careful diplomacy could, in fact, mitigate the harshness of Versailles. He secured a reduction in the total reparation demanded and payments could now be stretched over 60 years, rather than 30 as had been stipulated in the Treaty of Versailles.

Gustav Stresemann (1878–1929), foreign minister between 1923 and 1929, was Germany's most successful politician of the 1920s. He managed to win back the trust of most of Germany's old enemies and renegotiate the reparation payments.

The Nazis lost their appeal. Just how weak the party was became clear in the elections of 1928. The Nazis gained only 2.6 percent of the votes, fewer even than in 1924. The Social Democratic Party gained nearly 30 percent and the conservative National People's Party 14 percent. The Nazis' poor showing at this election earned them a mere twelve deputies in the Reichstag. Goebbels and Gregor Strasser were among them.

Göring and Himmler

Despite the weakness of the party, there were by now other important men in it who were to shape its future. One was Hermann Göring, a First World War air ace who had aristocratic connections that helped make Nazism seem much more respectable than it really was. Göring saw himself as a daredevil who brought glamour to the party. His first involvement with the Nazis was in the early 1920s as the head of the Stormtroopers. After the failure of the Beerhall Putsch he had left Germany, but Hitler had asked him to return to run for election, and he was one of the twelve elected deputies in 1928. Intensely loyal to Hitler, he was now one of the most important figures in the party.

More sinister was Heinrich Himmler. Himmler was conscientious, hardworking and ambitious, but displayed few leadership qualities. However, he was virulently anti-Semitic and obsessed with the superiority and purity of the German race. Hitler found a place for him as head of his unit of bodyguards, the SS. Himmler gave this unit a black uniform to distinguish it from the brownshirted Stormtroopers, and enforced firm discipline. The SS was now the party's secret police, ready to gather information about threats to Hitler and, when ordered to do so, to deal with them brutally.

Heinrich Himmler (1900–1945) was one of the most unlikely members of the Nazi elite. The son of a schoolmaster, he had the air of a dull administrator. However, Hitler noted his fanatical anti-Semitism and cold ruthlessness, and made him the first head of the notorious SS. He went on to become one of the key figures behind the extermination of the Jews.

HOW DID IT HAPPEN?

Was Germany ever stable?

Many historians stress the stability of Germany between 1924 and 1929. As Ian Kershaw puts it:

'These were Weimar's "golden years" … in the economy, industrial production came to surpass the pre-war level for the first time. Real wages did the same. The welfare state made impressive progress. Health provision was far superior to the pre-war period. Public spending on housing increased massively … the first glimmers of a mass-consumer society were visible…'

However, at street level it was not so calm. An Englishman, Christopher Isherwood, records his own memories of Berlin in the 1920s:

'Berlin was in a state of civil war. Hate exploded suddenly, without warning, out of nowhere; at street corners, in restaurants, cinemas, dance halls, swimming baths; at midnight, after breakfast, in the middle of the afternoon. Knives were whipped out, blows were dealt with spiked rings, beer mugs, chair-legs or leaded clubs, bullets slashed the advertisements on the poster columns…'

Ian Kershaw, *Hitler:1889–1936, Hubris* (Allen Lane, Penguin, 1998)
Christopher Isherwood, *The Berlin Stories* (New Directions Publishing Corporation, 1954)

4 Achieving Power: 1929–33

In 1929, disaster hit Germany once again. After years of boom in the 1920s, in October the New York Stock Exchange saw panic selling as confidence in the US economy fell. Much of the revival of the German economy had been based on short-term loans from American banks. Now these loans were called back to America, leading to a collapse in the German economy. Industrial production fell by 40 percent in 3 years, and unemployment soared.

Voting Patterns in the Weimar Republic

Parties	Percentage of total votes cast in elections						
	1920 June	1924 Dec.	1928 May	1930 Sept.	1932 July	1932 Nov.	1933 March
Communist	2.1	9.0	10.6	13.1	14.5	16.9	12.3
Social Democratic	21.7	26.0	29.8	24.5	21.6	20.4	18.3
Centre	13.6	13.6	12.1	11.8	12.5	11.9	11.2
National People's	15.1	20.5	14.2	7.0	6.2	8.9	8.0
Nazis	–	3.0	2.6	18.3	37.4	33.1	43.9

This table of voting patterns shows the rise of the Nazis; in 1920 they had no support, yet by 1933 they had become the largest political party in Germany. While the communists and Social Democrats maintained the core of their votes, their refusal to work together to fight the Nazis meant that they were easily out-manoeuvred by Hitler after 1933.

The Depression

Confronted with this crisis, the Weimar government was shown to be powerless. The capable foreign minister, Gustav Stresemann, died in October. In 1930, the new leading minister or chancellor, as he was known, was Heinrich Brüning from the Catholic Centre Party. His party had secured only 12 percent of the votes in the 1928 elections, so Brüning had to try to rule through a coalition of parties. This plan did not work, and the sessions of the Reichstag became so rowdy that the Reichstag limited its own meetings. In the years before 1930 it had met for an average of some 100 days a year. Between October 1930 and March 1931 it met for only 50 days, and then for only 24 days between April 1931 and June 1932. Between July 1932 and February 1933 it met for only 3 days. Instead of parliamentary democracy, Germany was ruled by decrees issued by the president, Paul von Hindenburg, the former military leader of Germany during the First World War.

Hitler Moves Forward

With the collapse of the economy and the erosion of parliamentary government, Hitler's party, which was small but well organized, was well placed to play on the old discontents and humiliations of Germany, which had been revived by the misery of the Depression. Hitler's overriding aim was power, and he did not care how he achieved it. He increased the number of his public speeches and adapted them to particular audiences.

Hitler proved brilliant at telling each group in German society that he had something to offer it. For example, one day he would promise farmers higher prices for their grain, and the next a workers' group cheaper bread. Few bothered to question how Germany could have both. Sixty percent of the Nazi voters were middle class, and Hitler promised them a revitalized economy with new job opportunities, the suppression of communism and a return to traditional German values of hard work and sober living. The communists, he argued, were not just disruptive and threatening to the middle class, they were under the control of a foreign power, the Soviet Union.

In July 1931, the Berlin Stock Exchange (pictured) was temporarily closed in order to avoid a panic on the markets during the banking crisis which followed the Depression. It was a powerful sign of just how crippled the Germany economy had become.

The Election of 1930

Once again, the Nazis proved especially popular among the farmers suffering from falling world prices. Hitler also reached out for the first time to businessmen – for whom he would switch from a Nazi uniform to a business suit. To them, too, he could promise the suppression of the workers and a more stable economy. In return they were now prepared to help finance a party which appeared to be their saviour.

Part of the appeal of the Nazis lay in their ability to offer unity against outsiders who threatened the German state. At home the communists and Jews were presented as the main enemies. Abroad it was those who had humiliated Germany at Versailles. The Nazis also scapegoated the Slav peoples of Eastern Europe, who had emerged from the collapse of the Russian and Austrian empires after World War One. The Nazis argued that they should be integrated into a greater Germany.

Just how effective the Nazis were became clear in the elections of September 1930. The Nazis won over 18 percent of the votes. They were now the second largest party after the Social Democratic Party, but the Social Democrats could not offer them much opposition. The workers who were its main supporters were demoralized by unemployment, and the party was also fighting off the challenge of the Communist Party, which preached revolution. The stronger the communists became, and they increased their votes in every election between 1920 and 1932, the more Hitler could present them as a threat to Germany.

Discipline and Display

If the Nazis were to capitalize on the chaos brought by the breakdown of German society in the Depression, it was vital that they themselves presented an image of disciplined power. This was achieved at the

This parade through the streets of Nuremberg shows how the Nazis used massed ranks of marchers and dramatic flags to create an impact. Some of the onlookers are giving a Nazi salute.

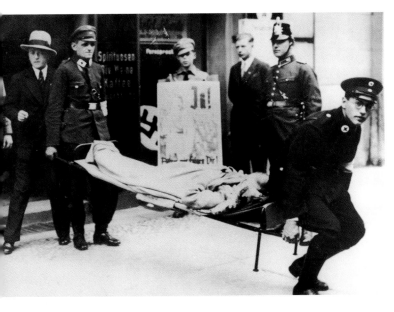

Unrest on the streets, particularly between Nazis and communists, was a major feature of Germany in the early 1930s. Here, a casualty is being carried away. The boy is displaying what appears to be an election poster for Hitler.

Nuremberg rallies, which were held every year from 1927. The ancient city of Nuremberg was a perfect setting against which to mix the old Germany with the new Germany the Nazis promised to create.

Every year, the rituals of the rally became more elaborate and emotional. Well over 100,000 party members might attend, many arranged in ranks in uniform and backed by rows of swastika-ed banners. A massive platform would dominate the parade ground, and once the party faithful and foreign guests who needed to be impressed

VOICES FROM THE PAST

Hidden truth

Nazism cloaked its underlying brutality under a mask of respectability. Albert Speer, a young architect and member of Hitler's inner circle, describes an example:

'What was decisive for me was a speech by Hitler which my students finally persuaded me to attend. From what I had read in the opposition press, I expected to find a screaming, gesticulating fanatic in uniform, instead of which we were confronted with a quiet man in a dark suit who addressed us in the measured tones of an academic.'

A letter written in 1953 by Speer to his daughter, quoted in Gitta Sereny, *Albert Speer: His Battle with Truth* (Macmillan, 1995)

VOICES FROM THE PAST

Songs on the streets

While moderates were attracted to the Nazi party in the belief that it would bring order, a very different mood was to be found among the Stormtroopers. This is from one of their songs:

> *'We are the Storm Columns, we put ourselves about,*
> *We are the foremost ranks, courageous in a fight,*
> *With sweating brows from work, our stomachs without food!*
> *Our calloused, sooty hands our rifles hold.*
>
> *So stand the Storm Columns, for racial fight prepared,*
> *Only when Jews bleed are we liberated,*
> *No more negotiation; it's no help, not even slight:*
> *Beside our Adolf Hitler we're courageous in a fight.'*

Richard Evans, *The Coming of the Third Reich* (Allen Lane, Penguin, 2003)

When the young Horst Wessel (1907–1930) was killed in Berlin in a brawl with communists Goebbels saw the chance to turn him into a martyr. The transformation of Wessel's verses into the Nazi anthem was typical of Goebbels' brilliant manipulation of events to the Nazis' advantage.

were assembled, Hitler would make his way up the central avenue to the solemn tone of a funeral march. In later rallies, rows of searchlights would point to the sky. Then, after dramatic salutes and shouts of *Heil Hitler*, Hitler's speech would begin. By now, he was a master of his craft. He would start slowly, gradually building up to an emotional crescendo: 'Is there anything left in Germany they [the Jews] haven't ruined?' was one impassioned climax.

On the streets of Germany's big cities the Stormtroopers, who appeared so disciplined at Hitler's rallies, would show a very different face: one of violent hatred towards rival parties and, above all, the communists. Their propaganda, however, skilfully concealed the reality. For example, when one party member, Horst Wessel, was shot in Berlin by communists after a dispute over a girl, he was hailed as a Nazi martyr. A song he had written – *The Flag's Held High* – was transformed by Goebbels into the Nazi anthem.

The Elections of 1932

Just how successful this propaganda had become was to be seen in the presidential elections of March 1932. Hindenburg, now an old man of 84, decided to run again, and Hitler (who by now had become a German citizen) challenged him. Hitler lost, but he won a staggering 13 million votes. He had drawn heavily on the discontent of a nation demoralized by the Depression. Four months later, in the Reichstag elections, the Nazis used every campaign strategy possible. Their posters appeared everywhere, their music blared from loudspeakers, Stormtoopers marched through the streets, and Hitler made visits all over Germany by plane. Although it was not clear how they would do it, the Nazis promised to solve the economic crisis.

The propaganda paid off: the Nazi vote doubled to 37.4 percent, making the Nazis the largest party, with 100 more seats than their nearest rivals, the Social Democrats. Hitler seemed unstoppable, and he now began to clamour that Hindenburg appoint him as chancellor.

Hindenburg, however, was reluctant to appoint a man he saw as an upstart. Moreover, he preferred to collaborate with his own choice for chancellor, a Catholic aristocrat, Franz von Papen. Papen's policy was to bypass parliamentary government altogether and rule through decree. It was soon clear that this policy had little support, but Hitler, too, seemed to be in trouble. The economy was beginning to revive and many were now beginning to see that the Nazi propaganda concealed a party that was responsible for much of the violence on the streets. In new elections in November, the Nazis actually lost 2 million votes, and their finances were suffering under the burden of so much electioneering.

All was not lost for them, however. By late 1932, the German government was in turmoil. The Reichstag was a battleground between the communists and the Nazis. Franz von Papen realized he had no support and resigned as chancellor in December. An army

This poster for the presidential election of 1932 reads, 'We want work and bread! Vote for Hitler!' Hitler did not achieve nearly enough votes to beat Hindenburg, but enough to dramatically demonstrate his growing popularity.

On 30 January 1933, President Hindenburg formally confirmed Hitler as chancellor. Few realized just how quickly Hitler would consolidate Nazi control of Germany.

TURNING POINT

The Depression

The Depression of 1929 to 1932 marked a turning point for Germany because it affected every class of society. The industrial workers suffered, as did middle-class people, severely affected by the collapse of banks. In the countryside, farmers suffered from low prices and agricultural workers were thrown off the large estates. The vitality of the Nazis seemed attractive at this time of despair.

general, Kurt von Schleicher, took over, but his only plan was to suppress the Nazis and declare a military government. Von Papen, angry at his loss of office, plotted an alternative. He would ask Hindenburg to make Hitler chancellor, surround him by von Papen's supporters, and hope to control the Nazis that way. On 30 January 1933, Hitler was finally appointed chancellor, and Von Papen told his supporters that he now had Hitler boxed in. He was wrong.

The evening of his appointment as chancellor, Hitler greeted the massed crowds of supporters from the chancellery window in Berlin. It soon became clear that this was no mere transfer of power from one chancellor to the next, but the start of a new era in German history.

HOW DID IT HAPPEN?

Why did the Nazis succeed?

Historian Klaus Fischer attributes the Nazis' success to the economic conditions of the time:

'The Nazi upsurge can be attributed primarily to the Depression that had ruined many German businesses and led to a tragic increase in unemployment. The Depression, in turn, stirred up a pervasive fear of impending political chaos, leading to an acute crisis in confidence for the democratic system … the Nazis were undoubtedly beneficiaries of popular anti-democratic feelings that they themselves did not create.'

By contrast, historian Wolfram Pyta argues that the Nazis' ability to play on a demoralized Germany's woes gained them popularity:

'The Nazi programme was skilfully tailored to winning the rural vote. It created a conservative image for itself by speaking up for the preservation of the rural way of life … it invoked the idea of a 'People's Community' transcending the classes which awoke a multitudes of hopes, particularly among parish priests and teachers who felt they were being taken seriously … the Nazis were the only party able to present an attractive offering to all village authorities.'

Klaus Fischer, *Nazi Germany* (Constable, 1995); Wolfram Pyta quoted in Neil Gregor (ed.), *Nazism* (Oxford University Press, 2000)

5 The Nazis Come to Power

When Hitler was appointed chancellor on 30 January 1933, he was determined to show that this was no ordinary political development. That same night, a vast parade was organized by Goebbels, the head of the party in Berlin, to march through the city. But politically Hitler looked weak. Only two other Nazis were appointed ministers and so it seemed at first as if the Nazis might successfully be contained. This is certainly what von Papen believed. However, one of the Nazis, Wilhelm Frick, was Minister of the Interior and the other, Hermann Göring, was made head of the police of Germany's largest state, Prussia. Between them they controlled law and order in Germany. Almost immediately they put in place plans to ban the Communist Party.

Hitler's first cabinet, shown here, had only two Nazis. One, sitting on Hitler's right, was Hermann Göring, police chief in Prussia. The other, shown directly behind Hitler, was Wilhelm Frick, the Minister of the Interior. The former chancellor, Franz von Papen, is sitting to Hitler's left.

VOICES FROM THE PAST

The march past

This eyewitness account of the event on 30 January 1933, by a teenage girl, Melita Maschman, shows the mixed emotions aroused by Nazism:

'For hours the columns marched by. Again and again amongst them we saw groups of boys and girls scarcely older than ourselves ... At one point somebody suddenly leapt from the ranks of the marchers and struck a man who had been standing only a few paces away from us, perhaps he had made a hostile remark. I saw him fall to the ground with blood streaming down his face and I heard him cry out. Our parents hurriedly drew us away from the scuffle, but they had not been able to stop us seeing the man bleeding. The image of him haunted me for days.

The horror it inspired in me was almost imperceptibly spiced with an intoxicating joy. "We want to die for the flag," the torchbearers had sung ... I was overcome with a burning desire to belong to these people for whom it was a matter of life and death ... I wanted to escape from my childish, narrow life and I wanted to attach myself to something that was great and fundamental.'

Richard Evans, *The Coming of the Third Reich* (Allen Lane, Penguin, 2003)

With political life in such disarray, the only institution that might have stood up to Hitler was the army. Hitler knew that many officers looked down on him as an upstart who, even after four years in the war, had risen to no higher rank than corporal, so he moved quickly. On 3 February, he met with the leading officers to promise that he would work to dismantle the Treaty of Versailles and rebuild the army. He even promised the army a specific role, to invade Eastern Europe in order to create a greater Germany in which the Slav inhabitants would be replaced by German settlers. The officers warmed to this chance to re-establish their status and made it clear that they would not intervene if Hitler consolidated his power.

The Breakdown of Law

Next, Hitler called for another election to be held on 5 March. Now that he had control of the police he could use them to intimidate the Nazis' opponents. The Nazi propaganda machine declared the communists to be enemies of Germany, and called for them and anyone who supported them to be destroyed.

This parade of political administrators held at Nuremberg in 1933 shows just how dominant a symbol the swastika had become. It is not only the central emblem of the flag, but is also worn as an armband by each man marching.

Raids against communist offices began soon after Hitler had come to power. This picture shows large quantities of papers being seized and taken off for destruction. All political life outside the Nazi Party was gradually extinguished.

TURNING POINT

The first official campaign against the Jews

Anti-Semitism had always been part of the Nazi ideology and the Stormtroopers freely denigrated the Jews in their marching songs. At the end of March 1933, very soon after the Nazis came to power, they organized a boycott of all Jewish businesses. On 1 April, all Jewish shops across Germany were closed, with Stormtroopers placed outside to make sure no one broke the ban. 'An imposing spectacle … a huge moral victory for Germany: we have shown everyone abroad that we can call on the whole nation for action,' wrote Goebbels in his diary. It seemed a small beginning, but it was the first step that led to the stripping of citizenship from Jews and eventually the extermination programmes of the Holocaust.

Communist and Social Democratic demonstrations were broken up and their party offices were vandalized. Newspapers supporting the Centre Party were closed down. Businessmen were told they must contribute to the Nazi election fund if they wanted the police to suppress strikes. In Prussia, Göring ordered the police to turn a blind eye to Nazi violence: 'Every bullet that now leaves the mouth of a police pistol is my bullet. If you call that murder, then I am the murderer, for I gave the order and stand by it.'

Many communists stood by as their party was destroyed. They had been told by their advisers in the Soviet Union that the very violence of the Nazis might bring about the workers' revolution. They had only to wait.

The Reichstag Fire

Then the Nazis had an extraordinary piece of luck. A young Dutchman, Marinus van der Lubbe, in despair at the ruthless behaviour of the Nazis, decided to launch a one-man protest. On the 27 February, he broke into the Reichstag building and set it on fire. Hitler, Göring and Goebbels were all in Berlin that night and they rushed to the scene. Hitler stared at the sea of flames and then burst out to his colleagues: 'There will be no more mercy now; anyone who stands in our way will be butchered. The German people will no longer understand leniency. Every communist functionary will be shot where he is found. The communist deputies must be hanged this very night. Everybody in league with the communists to be arrested. Against Social Democrats too there will be no mercy!'

Orders were put out at once to arrest leading communists, and 4,000 were rounded up and many dispatched to the first concentration camps. A law was drawn up that allowed Hitler's government to limit freedom of speech and the right to hold meetings, and to allow house searches

On 27 February 1933, the Reichstag building in Berlin was destroyed by fire. The fire proved a godsend to the Nazis, who could claim that the communists had been behind it.

The elections of March 1933 were to be the last Germany saw for many years. Even with massive intimidation, the Nazis failed to gain a full majority, but soon afterwards they enforced their dictatorship. Here the streets of Berlin are shown littered with election leaflets.

and the reading of mail. Freedoms and privacy rights once guaranteed by the Weimar Constitution were swept aside. Hindenburg, always suspicious himself of the communist workers' movement, was persuaded to sign the law.

The election of 5 March took place against a background of mounting hysteria. What was remarkable was that the Nazis won only 43.9 percent of the votes although, with the addition of another 8 percent from the National People's Party, which had agreed to support the Nazis, they did have a small majority. Despite all the propaganda against them, the communists and Social Democrats still managed to get 30 percent of the votes. Now everyone waited for 21 March when the new Reichstag would meet for the first time. It would be the first chance for the Nazis to exert their power.

HOW DID IT HAPPEN?

Accepting Nazi rule

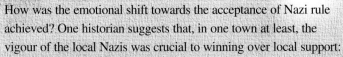

How was the emotional shift towards the acceptance of Nazi rule achieved? One historian suggests that, in one town at least, the vigour of the local Nazis was crucial to winning over local support:

'Thalburg's Nazis created their own image by their own initiative, vigour and propaganda. They knew exactly what needed to be done to effect the transfer of power to themselves in the spring of 1933 ... Hitler, Goebbels, and the other Nazi leaders provided the political decisions, ideology, national propaganda and, later, the control over the government which made the revolution possible. But it was in the hundreds of localities like Thalburg all over Germany that the revolution was made actual. They formed the foundation of the Third Reich.'

Others argue that Hitler was helped by exploiting the anti-communism of many Germans who were not otherwise Nazis:

'The long-standing hatred of Socialism and Communism was played upon by Nazi propaganda and turned into outright anti-communist paranoia. Pumped up by the Nazis, fear of a communist uprising was in the air. The closer the election came, the shriller grew the hysteria. The full-scale assault on the left was, therefore, sure of massive popular support...'

William Sheridan Allen, *The Nazi Seizure of Power: The Experience of a Single Town* (Eyre and Spottiswood, 1966); Ian Kershaw, *Hitler:1889–1936, Hubris* (Allen Lane, Penguin, 1998)

On election day in March 1933, members of the Berlin police lined up to vote. The only election poster shown is one of Hitler, who has cleverly portrayed himself with Hindenburg, as if he is the president's choice.

6 The Nazis Consolidate Power

On 21 March, the first day of spring, the Reichstag met for the first time since the Nazis had seized power. A service was held in one of Berlin's most hallowed churches, the Potsdam Garrison Church, where the Prussian kings lay buried. The Nazis organized a grand ceremony to make it look as if they were reaching back in an unbroken line to the great German war heroes of the past such as Frederick the Great.

Many observers had no illusions about Hitler. In this poster from the United States from about 1934, he is shown as a gorilla clutching the defenceless maiden, Germany. In his hand is a boulder labelled 'Intolerance'.

The Enabling Law

All may have been dignified on 21 March, but two days later things were very different. With the Reichstag in ashes, the first session of the new parliament was to be held in the Kroll Opera House. As the members assembled it was clear who was in charge. Most of the eighty-one communist deputies that had been elected had been arrested or otherwise prevented from attending. Stormtroopers and the SS were everywhere, even guarding the doors of the building once they had been shut for the beginning of proceedings. Great banners bearing the swastika hung from the walls. For centuries, the ancient symbol of the swastika had represented life and good luck. Once adopted by the Nazis it became a symbol of the Aryan, or dominant white race's, power.

Hitler, in a long and restrained speech, asked the Reichstag to pass a law, to be known as the Enabling Law, which would give him full control over government for four years. Hardly anyone spoke against it. The National People's Party, which had lost heavily to the Nazis in recent elections, supported it. The Catholic Centre Party was given some meaningless concessions in exchange for its votes. Only the Social Democrats made a last brave stand, their leader Otto Wells speaking firmly for principles of humanity, justice and freedom.

Hitler next showed his true personality. He tore into the Social Democrats with contempt: 'Germany will be free, but not through

VOICES FROM THE PAST
A promise to the German people

Hitler gave this speech on 10 February 1933, in which he asked for four years to prove himself. These four years were to be provided by the Enabling Law:

'For 14 years [i.e. 1919–33] the parties of disintegration, of the November Revolution, have seduced and abused the German people. For fourteen years they wreaked destruction, infiltration and dissolution. Considering this it is not presumptuous of me to stand before the nation today, and plead to it: German people give us four years and then pass judgement upon us, German people give us four years, and I swear to you, just as we, just as I have taken office, so shall I leave it ... I cherish the firm conviction that the hour will come at last in which the millions who despise us today will stand by us and with us will hail the new, hard-won and painfully acquired German Reich we have created together, the new German kingdom of greatness and power and glory and justice. Amen.'

Richard Evans, *The Coming of the Third Reich* (Allen Lane, Penguin, 2003)

Concentration camps were set up as soon as the Nazis came to power. Pacifists were among those imprisoned, notably Carl Von Ossietzky, a journalist and important peace activist even before 1933. Refusing to leave Germany, he was arrested the day after the Reichstag fire, and remained in concentration camps for most of the next five years. In 1936, he was awarded the Nobel Peace Prize, but the Nazis refused to allow the award to be reported in Germany. He died from tuberculosis in 1938.

you,' he shouted to the cheers of the Nazi deputies. The vote was then taken. Four hundred and forty-one deputies voted in favour, 94 – the Social Democrats – against. The next day the Enabling Law was in force. This was the moment when democracy disappeared under the Nazi tyranny. There was no longer a parliament through which the voice of the people could be heard.

The Crushing of Opposition

With the Weimar Constitution in tatters, the full power of Nazism was unleashed. Already, on the 22 March, the first concentration camps had been set up. They soon became the home of communists and other political opponents of the Nazis. Right from the start there was street-level violence against Jews. The move to exclude them from public life and their extermination followed inexorably.

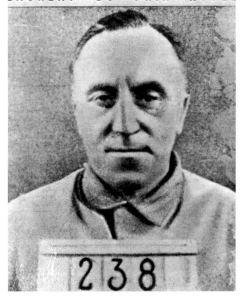

CET HOMME TRAQUÉ ÉTAIT LAURÉAT DU PRIX NOBEL

238

VOICES FROM THE PAST

A pledge to freedom

The leader of the Social Democratic Party, Otto Wels, spoke out against Hitler's Enabling Law:

> *'We the German Social Democratic Party pledge ourselves solemnly in this historic hour to the principles of humanity and justice, of freedom and socialism. No enabling act can give you the power to destroy ideas which are eternal and indestructible.'*

William L. Shirer, *The Rise and Fall of the Third Reich* (Secker & Warburg, 1960)

Book burning became an important public event in Nazi Germany, with texts by famous Jews and communists being targeted. In this picture from May 1933, Nazi officials and many civilians in the crowd give the Nazi salute over the ashes.

The Nazis needed to control any organization that might prove a threat to them: the trade unions were the first. On 1 May, the Nazis announced a workers' public holiday: a 'Day of National Labour'. A million workers were assembled on a field outside Berlin and many who had opposed the Nazi rise to power were horrified when they found themselves surrounded by Nazi banners. Their fears were justified. The very next day all German trade union offices were raided. All members were forced to place themselves under the control of the German Labour Front, which was a newly created Nazi version of a trade union.

The next step was to close down all political parties. The communists had already been banned, and the Social Democrats were next. On 21 June, the interior minister, Wilhelm Frick, ordered the banning of the party throughout Germany. 'The Social Democratic party has been dissolved. The total state won't have to wait for long now,' wrote Goebbels in his diary. The Centre Party was more difficult to deal with because of its deep roots in the Catholic Church. The Nazis, however, promised the Church that it would benefit from the Nazi campaign against communism and

TURNING POINT

The end of Weimar Democracy

The passing of the Enabling Law on 23 March gave Hitler the right to rule as he liked and from then on the Reichstag was only used when Hitler wanted to harangue the assembled Nazi deputies. He had only them to talk to because by the summer of 1933 all the other political parties had been banned, destroyed or forced to accept the dominance of the Nazis. Not only did the Nazis have full power, they were able to use it without any regard for human rights. A current of terror ran through German life and it was already clear that communists and Jews were to be the focus of the regime's hatred.

atheism, and it accepted Nazi rule. The party actually agreed to dissolve itself on 5 July 1933. The smaller political parties were soon bullied into submission, and the governments of the individual German states were also dissolved.

The Economic Programme

The repression was masked by a revival in the economy. Hitler, in fact, did not know or care much about economics. He had assumed that, in the long term, an expansion to the east would give Germany resources of land to enable it to be self-sufficient. However, he did implement two major programmes that helped provide new employment.

The first *Autobahn*, or motorway, was opened in May 1935. It ran from Munich to the Austrian border and, as the ranks of Nazis with flags on the bridge show, was treated as a propaganda victory for the new regime. It reinforced the image of the Nazis as masters of new technologies and engineering.

One was rearmament, or the resupply of weapons, which was promised secretly to the army because such a move was in direct breach of the Treaty of Versailles. Hitler did not want to rouse the suspicions of France and Britain at this early stage. The second was public works of housing and roads of which the *Autobahnen*, the motorways, grabbed the most headlines. As well as providing new jobs, the Autobahnen seemed to represent the new modern Germany that Hitler had promised. Because the Depression was coming to an end, in Europe at least, there was a new sense of economic well-being in Germany. Many were prepared to give credit for this to the Nazi regime and overlook its brutalities.

Hitler Crushes the Stormtroopers

Hitler's coming to power had excited the Stormtroopers who, under their leader Ernst Röhm, had assumed that they would have the pick of any new jobs and might even form the core of a new German army. Hitler, however, knew that he had to attract the existing army and state civil service whose support was vital if he was to administer Germany effectively and embark on rearmament. The Stormtroopers were being left without a role and their place in the party was further threatened when Göring began building up a new Nazi police force, the *Gestapo*. Leading Stormtroopers began to talk of a 'second revolution' which could place them at the centre of power.

Tensions between the party leaders and the Stormtroopers built up over several months until at last Hitler was persuaded to strike at Röhm and other Nazis who he believed threatened him. On the 'Night of the Long Knives', 30 June 1934, the SS with army support killed Röhm and about a hundred others. An emotional Hitler assembled the Reichstag to inform its members that he had been forced to become the judge for the German people. The Stormtroopers were subdued while the SS and the Gestapo tightened their control over the party and its enemies. The army now knew it had no rivals.

Only a few weeks later, on 2 August 1934, the aged president Hindenburg died. He had already been pushed aside by the Nazis, and Hitler now formally took over all his powers. The German army was forced to swear unconditional allegiance to 'Adolf Hitler, the *Führer* [leader] of the German nation and people.' Hitler had total power.

Why Did Hitler Succeed?

Hitler relied on the enthusiasm of his followers, the fear of the communists – which allowed him to destroy all human rights in the name of the German people – and the refusal of all but a few to oppose what was happening. Too many Germans turned a blind eye to the terror and intimidation, partly out of fear but partly because they thought these were incidental to the great programme of change and renewal that Hitler promised. After the upheavals and humiliations of the period since 1918, it was all too easy to succumb to a man who promised the restoration of German pride.

Hindenberg died on 2 August 1934, and is shown here shortly after his death. Hitler was now free to seize his powers, including that of commander-in-chief of the armed forces.

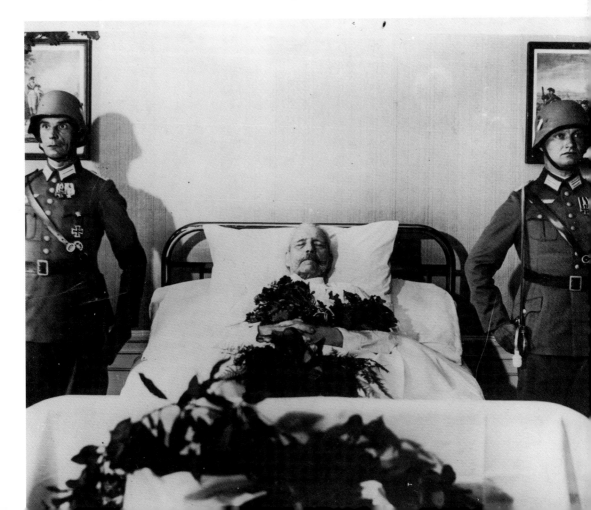

(Opposite) Nazi ceremonies became increasingly preoccupied with elaborate rituals. Here, from a rally of 1934, is the blessing of the flags. The display by the Nazis of swastikas on banners, emblems and armbands became commonplace, so that the image of the swastika soon became closely linked to the horror of Nazi rule.

HOW DID IT HAPPEN?

Nazi energy or a broken down system?

Historians disagree on the underlying reasons for Nazi success. Some, like William Carr, stress the dynamism of the Nazis:

'What was compelling about Hitler and what distinguished his party from other right-wing parties were not only the external trappings – the feverish activity, the endless marching, the mass rallies, and the ceaseless propaganda drives – important though these were in gathering votes, but above all the ruthless will to victory and fanatical sense of commitment emanating from the Führer and his followers.'

Others, including the veteran left-wing historian Eric Hobsbawm, blame the situation in Germany after the First World War:

'The best conditions for the triumph of the crazy ultra-Right were an old state and its ruling mechanism which could no longer function; a mass of disenchanted, disorientated and discontented citizens who no longer knew where their loyalties lay; strong socialist movements threatening or appearing to threaten social revolution, but not actually in a position to achieve it; and a move of national resentment against the peace treaties of 1918–20.'

William Carr, *Hitler, A Study in Personality and Politics* (Edward Arnold, 1978); Eric Hobsbawm, *Age of Extremes: The Short Twentieth Century, 1914–1991* (Michael Joseph, 1994)

It was true that a policy of government building of roads and armaments led to more employment and a reviving economy, but this masked the reality of Nazi dictatorship. Historian Richard Evans sums up what was still to come in his book *The Coming of the Third Reich* (Allen Lane, Penguin, 2003): 'Now [with full control of Germany] the Nazis would set about constructing a racial utopia, in which a pure-bred nation of heroes would prepare as rapidly and as thoroughly as possible for the ultimate test of German racial superiority: a war in which they would crush their enemies and establish a new European order that would eventually come to dominate the world.'

The Rise of Nazism Timeline

1889
20 April: Hitler born in Braunau in Austria

1905–13 Hitler in Vienna. Moves to Munich in 1913

1914 Outbreak of First World War. Hitler joins the German army

1918 Germany suffers defeat in war. Unrest in major German cities

1919
June: Treaty of Versailles brings humiliation to Germany
July: Friedrich Ebert establishes the Weimar Constitution
September: Hitler attends a meeting of the German Workers' Party in Munich. He joins and soon builds a reputation as an orator

1920
February: The German Workers' Party is renamed the German National Socialist Workers' Party. This soon becomes shortened to Nazi

1921
July: Hitler establishes himself as leader of the Nazis

1923
July: Inflation hits Germany and leads to major recruit-ment to the Nazi Party and its Stormtroopers
November: Hitler launches the Beerhall Putsch in Munich. It fails and Hitler is arrested

1924 Hitler serves a few months in prison for his part in the *Putsch*. Here he writes *Mein Kampf*

1925–6 Hitler re-establishes his leadership of the Nazi Party and starts creating a nationwide party. A return of economic stability to Germany hampers the party's growth

1928 Elections show the continuing weakness of the party. It achieves only 2.6 percent of the votes, and 12 seats in the Reichstag

1929 The stock market crash in New York leads to US loans being withdrawn from Germany and a major economic depression

1930 The Nazis exploit the unrest so well that they win 18.3 percent of the vote in the elections and 107 seats

1932 Continuing high unemployment and despair in Germany
April: Hitler runs against Hindenburg in the presidential election and wins 13 million votes
July: Elections make the Nazis the largest party in the Reichstag with 230 seats
November: New elections. The Nazis lose ground as voters turn against their violence

1933
January: Hitler is made chancellor in an attempt to contain him within a conservative government
February: Hitler orders new elections, and uses The Reichstag fire to justify human rights restrictions and anti-communism. He promises rearmament
March: In the elections, the Nazis win 43.9 percent of the votes. Hitler forces through an Enabling Law giving him absolute power
April: A boycott of Jewish businesses is imposed
July: With all political parties dissolved, Germany is, in effect, a one-party state

1934
June: In the 'Night of the Long Knives' Hitler destroys the Stormtrooper leadership and eliminates opponents
August: After Hindenburg's death, Hitler takes over all his powers. He becomes commander-in-chief of the German armed forces

Glossary

anti-Semitism Religious and racial prejudice against Jews.

Centre Party A moderate, conservative party, closely linked to the Catholic Church.

chancellor The leading minister under the Weimar Constitution, chosen by the president.

coalition government A government made up of an alliance between political parties.

communism A political movement advocating the equal division of resources.

Depression, the The worldwide economic collapse between 1929 and 1932, which hit Germany especially hard.

dictatorship A state under the domination of a single leader, as Germany became after 1933.

Enabling Law A law passed by the Reichstag in March 1933 enabling Hitler to rule without the Reichstag or other restraint.

fascism Italian political movement founded by Benito Mussolini in the early 1920s that shared many values with the Nazis, including anti-democratic beliefs.

Führer Leader.

Gestapo A Nazi police force established by Göring in Prussia.

Heil Hitler Formal greeting for Hitler, later used in everyday life as a sign of party loyalty.

inflation A general increase in prices and fall in the purchasing value of money.

National People's Party A conservative party with its roots in rural Germany. It shared many Nazi beliefs and supported Hitler in the passing of the Enabling Law.

Nazi Abbreviation of Nazionalsozialistische Deutsche Arbeiterpartei, German for National Socialist German Workers' Party.

proportional representation An election system in which seats are allocated to parties in proportion to the number of votes they gain.

Reichstag German parliament.

Social Democratic Party Non-communist left-wing party.

Stormtroopers Uniformed Nazi party members used to keep order and intimidate opponents. Also known as the SA from their German name *Sturmabteilung* or 'brownshirts'.

SS (*Schutzstaffel*) Founded as Hitler's bodyguards, they later became a major instrument of repression and terror.

Third Reich The name given to Hitler's state to link it to two earlier German 'Reichs' or states: those of Charlemagne, the first Holy Roman Emperor, and Bismarck, the creator of the unified German state (1871).

Weimar Constitution The German system of democratic government from 1919–33.

Further Information

Books:

Evans, David and Jenkins, Jane, *Years of the Weimar Republic and the Third Reich* (Hodder and Stoughton, 1998)

Evans, Richard, *The Coming of the Third Reich* (Allen Lane, Penguin, 2003)

Fest, J., *The Face of the Third Reich* (Penguin, 1979)

Hinton, C. and Hite, J., *Weimar and Nazi Germany* (John Murray, 2000)

Kershaw, Ian, *Hitler, 1889–1936* (Allen Lane, Penguin, 1998)

Lee, S., *Hitler and Nazi Germany* (Routledge, 1998)

Stone, Norman, *Hitler* (Coronet Books, 1989)

Wilmot, E., *Weimar and Nazi Germany* (Nelson Thornes, 1997)

Websites:

http://www.SchoolHistory.co.uk

http://www.historylearningsite.co.uk

http://www.spartacus.schoolnet.co.uk

http://www.Historyonthenet.com

Index   Numbers in **bold** refer to pictures